What can you do with balloons?

Written by Katie Foufouti

Illustrated by Ángeles Peinador

Collins

sky

airship

thin

long

shiny

Balloons are fun! They come in many different colours, shapes and sizes. There are round balloons, long balloons, balloons in animal shapes, balloons in car shapes.

There are always balloons at birthday parties. They make the house pretty and children love playing games with balloons.

These children are trying to catch the balloon in a paper cup. It's a difficult game, but they're having lots of fun. What other games with balloons do you know?

Look at these balloons. They're very long and thin. The funny person is using them to make lots of different animals. The children love them!

She makes a yellow dog, a blue snake and a green tiger with the balloons. What animal is she making now?

These balloons are shiny and we fill them with helium. The helium makes them go up in the sky.

These big balloons sometimes fly away from you! It's a good idea to hold them with two hands.

In the summer, children have fun with water balloons. They're small and you can put water in them.

The children are throwing the water
balloons at each other and they are
getting wet. What a great game!

Some balloons are bigger than the balloons we play with. In some cities, there are big balloons like this one. Children can't play with it. So what is it for?

There's writing on this balloon. On other balloons there's sometimes a camera.

Here's another big balloon with helium. Every day, people around the world send balloons like this up in the sky.

What for?

A weather balloon goes up to the sky.

They are weather balloons. They collect information about the weather in a small box. The balloon pops in the sky and the box falls to the ground.

This is an airship. An airship is a very big balloon with an engine. In the past, before there were big planes, people travelled in airships.

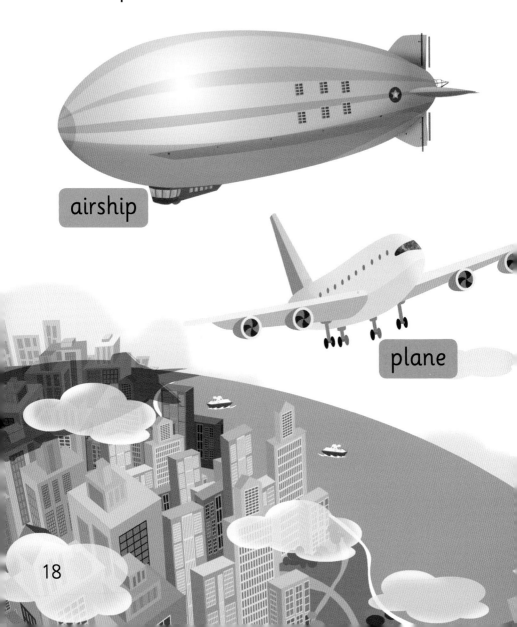

airship

plane

There are airships today, but people don't travel in them. They put writing on them or cameras in them. The cameras take photos of the city.

Look at these pretty balloons! We put hot air in these balloons and we call them 'hot air balloons'. There's a big basket under each hot air balloon. What is it for?

You can stand inside the basket and go for
a ride. The basket can carry eight people.
Where would you like to go in a hot
air balloon?

Picture dictionary

Listen and repeat

basket

game

long

shiny

sky

thin

wet

pop

1 Look and say the changes.

2 Listen and say

Collins

Published by Collins
An imprint of HarperCollins*Publishers*
Westerhill Road
Bishopbriggs
Glasgow
G64 2QT

HarperCollins*Publishers*
1st Floor, Watermarque Building
Ringsend Road
Dublin 4
Ireland

William Collins' dream of knowledge for all began with the publication of his first book in 1819.

A self-educated mill worker, he not only enriched millions of lives, but also founded a flourishing publishing house. Today, staying true to this spirit, Collins books are packed with inspiration, innovation and practical expertise. They place you at the centre of a world of possibility and give you exactly what you need to explore it.

© HarperCollins*Publishers* Limited 2020

10 9 8 7 6 5 4 3 2

ISBN 978-0-00-839837-8

Collins® and COBUILD® are registered trademarks of HarperCollins*Publishers* Limited

www.collins.co.uk/elt

British Library Cataloguing in Publication Data

A catalogue record for this publication is available from the British Library.

Author: Katie Foufouti
Illustrator: Ángeles Peinador (Beehive)
Series editor: Rebecca Adlard
Publishing manager: Lisa Todd
Product managers: Jennifer Hall and Caroline Green
In-house editor: Alma Puts Keren
Project manager: Emily Hooton
Editor: Frances Amrani
Proofreaders: Natalie Murray and Michael Lamb
Cover designer: Kevin Robbins
Typesetter: 2Hoots Publishing Services Ltd
Audio produced by id audio, London
Reading guide author: Emma Wilkinson
Production controller: Rachel Weaver
Printed and bound by: GPS Group, Slovenia

Download the audio for this book and a reading guide for parents and teachers at www.collins.co.uk/839837